FOR JENNIFER ANNE MESSING

A fragrant flower,
blossoming

A LIGHT ON THE PATH

published by Gold'n'Honey Books
a part of the Questar publishing family

©1996 by L. J. Sattgast
Illustrations ©1996 by Nancy Munger

Design by David Uttley

International Standard Book Number: 0-88070-913-8

Printed in the United States of America

For information:
Questar Publishers, Inc. • Post Office Box 1720 • Sisters, Oregon 97759

96 97 98 99 00 01 02 03 — 10 9 8 7 6 5 4 3 2 1

A LIGHT
on the
PATH

*Proverbs
for Growing Wise*

BY L. J. SATTGAST

ILLUSTRATIONS BY NANCY MUNGER

Gold 'n'
Honey
BOOKS

The path of the righteous is like the first gleam of dawn,
shining ever brighter till the full light of day.

Do you want to be wise?
Then come in.
Are you tired of lies?
Then come in.
Have you always wanted
To know what is right?
Can you find your way
On the path at night?
Then turn your eyes
To the golden light—
It's time to begin.
Come in!

Treasure!

Wisdom, what is it?
It's treasure untold!
It's better than rubies
Or diamonds or gold!

For when you know God
And follow His ways,
Then you will be wise
The rest of your days!

PROVERBS 9:10
*The fear of the Lord is the beginning of wisdom,
and knowledge of the Holy One is understanding.*

The Naughty Ones

"Come," say the naughty ones,
"Let's play a little game.
Let's push him off his tricycle
And call his sister names!"

"Come," say the naughty ones,
"Let's pull a little prank.
Let's catch the neighbor's pussy cat
And throw it in the tank!"

"Come," say the naughty ones,
"Let's climb the neighbor's tree.
We'll fill our buckets with his fruit,
And no one else will see."

The naughty ones did everything
Without a care or thought.
They bragged about their shameful deeds
Until they all were …

Caught!

PROVERBS 1:10
My son, if sinners entice you, do not give in to them...
These men lie in wait for their own blood;
they waylay only themselves.

A Golden Ring

Don't be like
The little girl
Who fixed her hair
So it would curl.
When she dressed
To look her best,
She looked down
Upon the rest.

Though she had
Such pretty eyes,
She could tell
Some awful lies!
And her rosy lips
Would whisper
Naughty things
About her sister.

She was such
A pretty thing,
Kind of like
A golden ring
That is shiny
Bright and big…

Stuck on the nose
Of a barnyard pig!

PROVERB 11:22
*Like a golden ring in a pig's snout is a beautiful
woman who shows no discretion.*

Planting Seeds

If you plant
Some little seeds,
Then you'll have
To pull some weeds...

Give them water
Every day,
And keep the hungry
Birds away.

If you work
Instead of sleep,
You will have
A crop to reap.

PROVERBS 10:5

*He who gathers crops in summer is a wise son,
but he who sleeps during harvest
is a disgraceful son.*

Ant Parade

I saw a troop of ants go by
One sunny summer day.
They gathered up my picnic crumbs
And took them all away.

They marched up to the anthill
And carried them inside,
For that is where they store their food,
And that is where they hide.

No one told them what to do.
They all just seemed to know
That it was time to gather food
Before the winter snow.

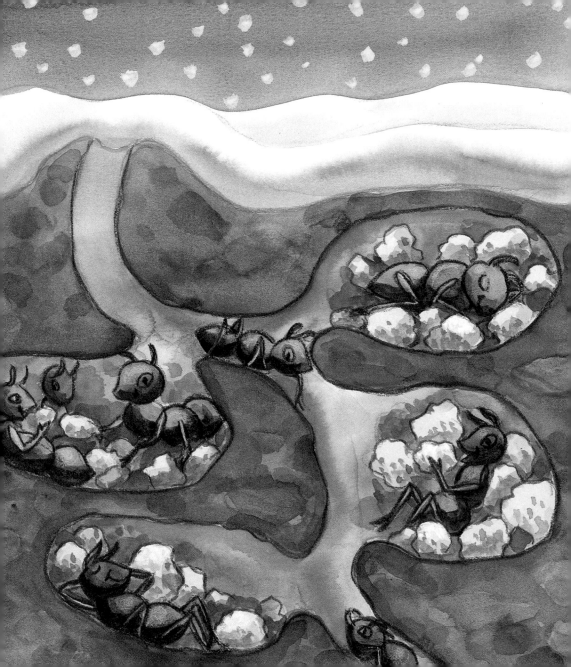

Wouldn't it be lovely
If we were just as bold
To do the things we ought to do
Before we're even told?

PROVERBS 6:6-8

Go to the ant, you sluggard.
Consider her ways and be wise! It has no commander,
no overseer or ruler, yet it stores its provisions in summer
and gathers its food at harvest.

The Secret

I heard a little secret
And promised not to tell,
But when I saw another friend,
I thought I might as well.

She told it to some others
Along the sandy shore,
And soon the little secret
Wasn't secret anymore.

PROVERBS 11:13
A gossip betrays a confidence,
but a trustworthy man keeps a secret.

Pennywise

Stingy! Stingy!
Won't give a penny.
When he tries to keep it all,
He hardly saves any.

Generous! Generous!
He will never lack.
The more he shares with others,
The more he gets back!

PROVERBS 11:24
One man gives freely, yet gains even more;
another withholds unduly,
but comes to poverty.

Listen!

Listen to your father, kids,
And please obey your mother.
Don't pull your sister's hair,
And never bite your brother.

When they say good morning,
Get up and make your bed.
Don't snuggle further down
And cover up your head.

Eat your food and brush your teeth
And wash your hands and face.
Hang your clothes up neatly,
And put your toys in place.

When it's time to go to bed,
Please turn out the light.
And don't forget to say your prayers
And kiss them both good night!

PROVERBS 1:8
*Listen, my son,
to your father's instruction and do not forsake
your mother's teaching.*

Lion in the Street

There's a lion outside!
Oh, I'm sure that he's there,
And he's probably hungry
And covered with hair
From the tip of his tail
To the end of his nose.
(He's waiting to have me
For lunch I suppose.)

And if I should happen
To open the door,
I know that he'll let out
A terrible ROAR!
Although I'm supposed to be
Mowing the lawn,
I'd much rather sit here
And wait till he's gone.
It shouldn't be more
Than an hour or two.
(By that time my favorite
Show will be through.)

So if you should wonder
And ask yourself why
The grass around here
Is incredibly high,
Just look all around
And I'm sure you will meet
The lion that's roaming
About on the street!

PROVERBS 26:13

The sluggard says, "There is a lion in the road,
a fierce lion roaming the streets!"

Trust in God

When you don't know what to do,
Trust in God.
When you're feeling sad and blue,
Trust in God.

When the answer isn't clear,
Just remember, God is near.
He will always see you through,
So trust in God!

PROVERBS 3 : 5, 6
Trust in the Lord with all your heart
and lean not on your own understanding.
In all your ways acknowledge him
and he shall direct your paths.

A Gentle Word

No need to holler,
No need to shout.
No need to wave
Your arms about.

Learn to speak
In a gentle way,
And watch the anger
Melt away.

PROVERBS 15:1

A gentle answer turns away wrath,
but a harsh word stirs up anger.

Linda Sue

Linda Sue,
What will you do
When mother says, "Come here!"
I'll say, "O.K."
And then I'll play
As though I didn't hear.

Linda Sue,
What will you do
When you are at the table?
I'll fuss and whine
Instead of dine
As long as I am able.

Linda Sue,
What will you do
When Dad says, "Time for bed!"
I'll sneak away
And start to play
Another game instead.

Linda Sue,
The things you do
Will bring your parents sorrow.
Lord, I see,
Please help me be
A better girl tomorrow.

PROVERBS 10:1
*A wise son brings joy to his father,
but a foolish son grief to his mother.*

Opposite Twins

Lazy Ike and careful Mike
Were look-alike brothers,
But lazy Ike and careful Mike
Were different from each other.

Lazy Ike would leave his bike
Lying on the ground,
While careful Mike would put his bike
Where it was safe and sound.

Lazy Ike would take a hike
Whenever there were chores,
But cheerful Mike said he would like
To help his parents more.

When it was time to give a dime
For every job well done,
Guess who stashed all the cash-
And guess which one got none?

PROVERBS 10:4
Lazy hands make a man poor,
but diligent hands bring wealth.

Words of Kindness

Hey, there! Say, there!
Have you any cheer?
Simple words of kindness
Are what I want to hear.

Bless you! Of course I do,
Let me fill your cup.
Simple words of kindness
Will cheer you right up!

PROVERBS 12:25
An anxious heart weighs a man down,
but a kind word cheers him up.

Big Spender

I got some money
From my Uncle Dan,
And I'm going to spend it
Just as fast as I can.

I'd like a game
And a cowboy hat,
Collector cards
And a baseball bat,
Some fishing gear
And a hockey stick,
And so much candy
It'll make me sick!

What did you say?
I should squirrel some away
And save it in case
I should need it someday?
Certainly not!
Though don't ask why…
Oh, what shall I,
What shall I,
What shall I buy?

PROVERBS 17:16
*Of what use is money in the hand of a fool
Since he has no desire to get wisdom?*

Friends

Choose your friends wisely
For soon you will see
That who you are with
Is what *you* will be.

PROVERBS 13:20
He who walks with the wise grows wise,
but a companion of fools suffers harm.

Don't Forget!

I've done my chores,
I've mopped the floors
And stirred my mother's stew.
But just before
I'm out the door,
There's one more thing to do.

My cat says, "Meow!
Please serve me now,
And fill my empty dish.
It suits me fine
At dinner time
To have my every wish!"

And then my pup
Starts jumping up
As he begins to bark,
"I'd like to run
And have some fun
While playing in the park!"

And there are yet
Some other pets
That I would never wanna
Forget to feed
or meet their needs,
From hamster to…

Iguana!

PROVERBS 12:10

*A righteous man
cares for the needs of his animal.*

Someone's Watching

When you wonder, "Should I dare?
No one sees and no one cares ,"
Just remember, God can see.
He is watching you and me.

PROVERBS 15:3
*The eyes of the Lord are everywhere,
keeping watch on the wicked and the good.*

Folly

Folly calls from far and near
To all the children who will hear:
"Come, I say, to everyone.
You deserve to have some fun!
You don't have to be polite.
Only sissies do what's right!"

If you listen to her voice,
You will make a dreadful choice,
For she's telling you a lie
That will surely make you cry!

PROVERBS 9:13–18
The woman Folly is loud;
She is undisciplined and without knowledge,
calling out to those who pass by,
"Let all who are simple come in here!"
But little do they know that the dead are there,
that her guests are in the depths of the grave.

Wisdom

Wisdom calls from far and near
To all the children who will hear:
"Don't be selfish, don't be rude,
Have a thankful attitude.
Learn to love what's right and good,
And always do the things you should!"

If you listen to her voice,
You will make a happy choice,
For she's telling you to do
What she knows is best for you.

And so, my friend,
Win or lose—
The time has come
For you to choose.

PROVERBS 9:1–11

Wisdom calls, "Let all who are simple come in here!
Leave your simple ways and you will live.
For through me your days will be many,
and years will be added to your life."